Safeguarding Against Crime in Everyday Life

C. P. Kumar
Reiki Healer & Author
Roorkee - 247667, India

Disclaimer

While every effort has been made to ensure the accuracy and completeness of the content in this book, the author cannot guarantee that the information contained herein is error-free, up-to-date, or suitable for every individual circumstance.

The author shall not be held liable or responsible for any errors or omissions in the content of the book, nor for any damages, or losses that may arise from any actions taken based upon the suggestions or contents presented in the book.

Readers are advised to use their own judgment and discretion in applying the information provided in this book, and to consult with qualified professionals before taking any action based on the contents of this book. The author disclaims any and all liability or responsibility for any actions taken or not taken based on the information contained in this book.

DEDICATION

To those who strive for a safer world,

This book is dedicated to the vigilant souls committed to the pursuit of safety in our everyday lives. It is an acknowledgment of the countless individuals who understand that safeguarding against crime is not merely a responsibility but a collective aspiration for a harmonious society.

In the spirit of shared responsibility, this dedication extends to those who dedicate their lives to preventing and combating crime - law enforcement officers, community leaders, educators, and every citizen who actively contributes to the safety of their community.

May the insights within these pages empower each reader with knowledge, awareness, and the tools necessary to navigate the intricacies of an ever-changing landscape. As we delve into the diverse chapters encompassing personal safety, crime prevention, and community well-being, let this dedication serve as a reminder that our collective efforts are the bedrock upon which a safer and more secure future is built.

Here's to a world where each step is taken with confidence, where communities are resilient, and where the dedication to safeguarding against crime becomes a shared ethos that transcends boundaries.

In dedication to a safer tomorrow,

C. P. Kumar

CONTENTS

PREFACE

In the tapestry of our daily lives, the threads of crime are unfortunately woven into the fabric of our existence. The impact of criminal activities reverberates through society, leaving indelible marks on individuals, families, and communities. "Safeguarding Against Crime in Everyday Life" is a comprehensive exploration of strategies and practices aimed at fortifying ourselves against the myriad challenges posed by crime.

This book embarks on a journey through the multifaceted landscape of crime, from understanding its pervasive nature to equipping individuals with the knowledge and tools needed to protect themselves and their loved ones. The chapters within delve into various realms of personal and communal safety, offering a wealth of information that empowers readers to navigate the complexities of a world where crime often lurks in unexpected corners.

The initial chapters cast a discerning eye on the broader canvas of crime, defining its contours and illustrating its far-reaching impact on society. A survey of crime statistics and trends serves as a compass, guiding readers through the ever-evolving nature of threats that surround us.

From personal safety to cybersecurity, each subsequent chapter provides practical insights and actionable strategies. Whether it's recognizing potential dangers, defusing confrontations, or securing our digital personas, the book addresses a spectrum of concerns with a focus on proactive prevention.

The diversity of topics covered reflects the holistic approach needed to address the myriad forms of crime.

Whether it's assault prevention, fraud awareness, or safeguarding against blackmail, the book recognizes that each facet of personal safety is interconnected, requiring a comprehensive understanding and a nuanced set of skills.

In addition to individual safety, this book extends its gaze to broader arenas, examining how communities can come together to create environments that resist criminal influences. Initiatives such as community policing, conflict resolution, and youth education form crucial components of our collective effort to foster responsible behavior and reduce the prevalence of crime.

The concluding chapter serves not only as a recapitulation of key strategies but as a rallying call for collective action. As we navigate the challenges of our modern world, the importance of community involvement and awareness cannot be overstated. By inspiring a culture of responsibility and safety, we lay the foundation for a future where individuals are not merely survivors but active participants in creating safer, more secure communities.

This book is not a panacea for all the ills of crime, but it is a guide - an invitation to explore, learn, and apply the principles that can empower us to lead safer lives. As we embark on this journey together, let us forge a path toward a future where the shadows of crime are diminished, and the light of safety illuminates our shared existence.

C. P. Kumar
Reiki Healer & Author
Former Scientist 'G', National Institute of Hydrology
Roorkee - 247667, India
Web: https://www.angelfire.com/nh/cpkumar/virgo.html

Introduction

Crime is a ubiquitous phenomenon that has persisted throughout human history, taking on various forms and evolving alongside societal changes. As we navigate the intricate web of human behavior, it becomes imperative to delve into the landscape of crime, dissecting its dimensions and exploring its profound impact on society. This article aims to provide a comprehensive overview of crime, its definitions, statistical trends, and the broader implications it has on our communities.

Defining Crime and its Impact on Society

Crime, at its core, is a violation of societal norms and laws. It encompasses a spectrum of activities that range from petty theft to heinous acts of violence. Defining crime is a complex task, as it is influenced by cultural, historical, and legal perspectives. From a legal standpoint, crime is often classified into two categories: felonies and misdemeanors. Felonies involve more severe offenses and carry heavier penalties, while misdemeanors are considered less serious infractions.

The impact of crime on society is multifaceted, affecting individuals, communities, and institutions. Beyond the immediate victims, crime breeds fear and erodes trust within communities. It disrupts the social fabric by creating a sense of insecurity and vulnerability. Moreover, crime places a significant burden on law enforcement agencies, judicial systems, and healthcare services, diverting resources away from other critical areas.

Understanding crime's impact requires an exploration of its psychological consequences on victims. Beyond physical harm, victims often grapple with emotional trauma, anxiety, and a diminished sense of safety. This ripple effect extends to families, friends, and neighbors, creating a collective unease that lingers long after the criminal act has occurred.

Overview of Crime Statistics and Trends

To comprehend the landscape of crime, we must turn our attention to crime statistics and trends. These data provide valuable insights into the prevalence and nature of criminal activities, allowing policymakers, law enforcement agencies, and researchers to develop informed strategies.

Crime statistics are typically collected and analyzed by government agencies, such as the Federal Bureau of Investigation (FBI) in the United States, and international organizations like INTERPOL. These statistics cover a wide array of offenses, including property crimes, violent crimes, white-collar crimes, and cybercrimes.

Violent crimes, such as homicide, assault, and robbery, are among the most scrutinized categories due to their severe impact on individuals and communities. Property crimes, including burglary and theft, also contribute significantly to the overall crime landscape. White-collar crimes involve non-violent, financially motivated offenses committed by individuals, businesses, or government professionals. The rise of technology has given birth to cybercrimes, a rapidly growing category encompassing a range of illicit activities conducted online.

Trends in crime often reflect broader societal shifts. Economic downturns, social unrest, and technological advancements can all influence the prevalence and nature of criminal activities. For example, periods of economic hardship may lead to an increase in property crimes as individuals face financial strain. Similarly, advancements in technology have given rise to new forms of crime, such as identity theft and cyber fraud.

Analyzing crime trends also requires an exploration of geographical variations. Certain regions may experience higher rates of specific crimes due to socioeconomic factors, cultural influences, or historical legacies. Understanding these regional variations is crucial for tailoring effective crime prevention and intervention strategies.

Conclusion

The landscape of crime is a dynamic and intricate tapestry woven into the fabric of human society. Defining crime involves navigating legal, cultural, and historical perspectives, while understanding its impact requires a recognition of the far-reaching consequences on individuals and communities. Crime statistics and trends provide a lens through which we can examine the prevalence and nature of criminal activities, offering valuable insights for policymakers and law enforcement agencies.

As we navigate the complex terrain of crime, it is essential to recognize that addressing this issue requires a multi-faceted approach. Prevention, intervention, and rehabilitation efforts must work in tandem to create a safer and more secure society. By understanding the dimensions of crime and its impact, we can strive towards building communities that are resilient, informed, and equipped to address the challenges posed by criminal activities. In this endeavor, the collaborative efforts of individuals, communities, and institutions are essential for fostering a society where the landscape of crime is continually reshaped towards a more just and secure future.

The opening chapter sets the stage for a comprehensive exploration of crime and its myriad facets. By delving into the landscape of crime, we equip ourselves with the knowledge needed to navigate this intricate terrain. As we venture into the subsequent chapters, we will unravel specific strategies and practices aimed at preventing and mitigating various forms of criminal activity. Together, we can empower individuals, families, and communities to forge a safer future.

Introduction

In an increasingly dynamic and unpredictable world, personal safety has become a paramount concern for individuals of all walks of life. Assaults and acts of violence can happen unexpectedly, and being prepared to protect oneself is crucial. This article delves into the various strategies for assault prevention, covering the importance of recognizing and avoiding potentially dangerous situations, exploring self-defense techniques, and ultimately emphasizing the significance of a proactive approach to personal safety.

Recognizing and Avoiding Potentially Dangerous Situations

1. Situational Awareness

Situational awareness forms the bedrock of personal safety. Understanding one's surroundings and being attuned to potential threats is key. This involves staying present and vigilant, avoiding distractions like excessive use of smartphones or headphones when in public spaces. By cultivating situational awareness, individuals can preemptively identify and sidestep potential danger.

2. Trusting Instincts

Often, our instincts provide valuable insights into a situation. Trusting one's gut feeling can be instrumental in avoiding danger. If a place or person feels unsettling, it's essential to heed those internal warnings and take appropriate action. This might involve changing direction, seeking help, or leaving the vicinity altogether.

3. Social Awareness

In social situations, recognizing red flags in interactions can be pivotal. Unsettling body language, inappropriate comments, or a general sense of discomfort can be warning signs. Being assertive in setting boundaries and disengaging from potentially harmful encounters is an essential skill in personal safety.

Self-Defense Techniques

1. Empowerment through Education

Education is a powerful tool in self-defense. Understanding basic self-defense techniques equips individuals with the confidence and skills needed to protect themselves. Workshops, courses, or online resources that focus on practical self-defense maneuvers empower individuals to react effectively in threatening situations.

2. Martial Arts Training

Martial arts training not only enhances physical fitness but also instills discipline and confidence. Techniques learned in disciplines such as karate, jiu-jitsu (Japanese martial arts), or krav maga (Israeli martial art) can be valuable assets in self-defense. Regular practice builds muscle memory, enabling individuals to respond instinctively and decisively when faced with an imminent threat.

Advancements in technology have given rise to various personal safety devices designed to provide individuals with an added layer of protection. From pepper sprays to personal alarms and mobile apps that can notify emergency services, these tools can offer peace of mind and act as effective deterrents.

Conclusion

Assault prevention is a multifaceted endeavor that requires a combination of awareness, education, and proactive measures. Recognizing and avoiding potentially dangerous situations, coupled with the acquisition of self-defense techniques, form a robust approach to personal safety.

By cultivating situational awareness and trusting instincts, individuals can navigate their surroundings with greater confidence. Social awareness is crucial in identifying and responding to red flags in interpersonal interactions, ensuring that boundaries are established and respected.

Empowerment through education is a fundamental aspect of assault prevention. Knowledge is a potent defense, and investing time in learning basic self-defense techniques can make a significant difference. Martial arts training goes a step further, not only enhancing physical capabilities but also fostering mental resilience and confidence.

Additionally, the advent of personal safety devices offers practical tools for individuals to carry with them, further bolstering their sense of security. From traditional items like pepper sprays to modern technologies like mobile apps, these devices contribute to a comprehensive personal safety strategy.

In essence, assault prevention is not a one-size-fits-all solution but a personalized, proactive approach to personal safety. By integrating these strategies into daily life, individuals can significantly reduce the risk of becoming victims of assault and contribute to creating safer communities. Empowering individuals with the knowledge and skills to protect themselves is an investment in building a society where personal safety is a shared priority.

Introduction

In an era where personal safety is a growing concern, it's crucial to equip ourselves with the knowledge and practices to prevent potential threats, especially in high-risk situations like robberies. The fear of falling victim to such crimes can be unnerving, but by adopting effective preventative measures, one can significantly reduce the likelihood of becoming a target.

Safe Practices for Handling Money and Valuables

1. Secure Payment Methods

The way we handle money in public spaces plays a pivotal role in deterring potential robbers. Opting for secure payment methods such as credit cards, mobile payments, or digital wallets minimizes the need to carry large sums of cash. This not only safeguards your finances but also eliminates the temptation for thieves.

2. Inconspicuous Valuables

Avoid drawing unnecessary attention by keeping valuable items discreet. Consider using inconspicuous bags or cases for items like laptops, cameras, or other expensive gadgets. The less conspicuous your valuables appear, the less likely you are to attract the attention of individuals with malicious intent.

3. Securing Your Home

Robbery prevention isn't just about personal safety in public spaces; it's also about securing your residence. Ensure that your home is equipped with reliable locks on doors and windows. Invest in a home security system that includes surveillance cameras and alarms, acting as a deterrent for potential intruders.

Awareness and Situational Alertness

1. Stay Alert in Public Spaces

One of the most effective ways to prevent a robbery is to remain aware of your surroundings. Avoid distractions like excessive phone use or listening to loud music, as these can hinder your ability to detect potential threats. Instead, stay vigilant and take notice of the people and activities around you.

2. Trust Your Instincts

Intuition is a powerful tool for self-preservation. If something feels off or makes you uncomfortable, trust your instincts and take appropriate action. Whether it's crossing the street, entering a store, or changing your route, following your gut feelings can often prevent a potentially dangerous situation.

3. Plan Your Routes

When navigating through high-risk areas, plan your routes in advance. Opt for well-lit and populated pathways, avoiding dark alleys or isolated areas. Familiarize yourself with emergency exits and public spaces where you can seek help if needed. A well-thought-out plan enhances your ability to respond quickly and effectively in case of an emergency.

4. Personal Security Devices

Consider carrying personal security devices such as personal alarms, pepper spray, or even self-defense tools if legal and appropriate. While the hope is never to use them, having such tools at your disposal can provide an extra layer of security and confidence, acting as a deterrent to potential assailants.

Conclusion

In a world where crime rates are unpredictable, taking proactive measures for robbery prevention is a responsibility we owe ourselves. By adopting safe practices for handling money and valuables, maintaining awareness and situational alertness, and incorporating these habits into our daily lives, we can significantly reduce the risk of falling victim to robberies.

Personal safety is a multifaceted endeavor that extends beyond individual actions. Communities, law enforcement, and society as a whole play crucial roles in fostering an environment where crime prevention is a shared goal. As we strive to make our lives safer, it's essential to contribute to the collective effort of creating a society where everyone can move freely without fear.

In conclusion, robbery prevention is not just about safeguarding our possessions; it's about protecting ourselves and our communities. By staying informed, staying alert, and being proactive in adopting preventative measures, we empower ourselves to navigate the world with confidence and security. Remember, the first step towards a safer future is the commitment to prioritize personal safety and the well-being of those around us.

Introduction

In the bustling landscapes of modern cities, the threat of quick theft, commonly known as snatching, has become an ever-present concern for individuals navigating public spaces. The sudden and forceful nature of snatch thefts can leave victims shocked and disoriented, making it crucial to explore effective deterrence strategies. This article delves into the art of minimizing the risk of quick theft, focusing on proactive measures that individuals can adopt to safeguard their belongings and personal safety.

Reacting to Snatch Attempts Without Escalating Violence

The first line of defense against snatch theft is understanding how to react in the moment. While it's a natural instinct to resist when someone tries to forcibly take your possessions, it is crucial to prioritize personal safety over material belongings. Reacting impulsively can escalate the situation, leading to potential harm.

1. Stay Calm and Assess the Situation

Reacting with panic can hinder your ability to make rational decisions. Take a deep breath, assess the situation quickly, and gauge the level of threat. Maintaining composure is key to making informed choices.

2. Let Go of Possessions

While it may be difficult to part with personal items, especially valuables, letting go can prevent physical harm. Remember that material possessions can be replaced, but injuries may have more lasting consequences.

3. Be a Vocal Assertor, Not an Aggressor

Verbal assertiveness can be a powerful deterrent. Shout for help, draw attention to the situation, and use a confident tone to dissuade the thief. However, avoid using aggressive language or making physical threats, as this may escalate the confrontation.

4. Create Distance Safely

Once you've let go of your belongings, focus on creating distance between yourself and the assailant. Move away calmly, keeping an eye on your surroundings to avoid potential follow-up attempts.

Securing Personal Items in Public

Prevention is the cornerstone of minimizing the risk of snatch theft. By adopting proactive measures and cultivating situational awareness, individuals can significantly reduce their vulnerability in public spaces.

1. Use Anti-Theft Bags

Investing in anti-theft bags equipped with features like lockable zippers, slash-resistant straps, and RFID-blocking compartments adds an extra layer of protection. These specialized bags are designed to thwart quick theft attempts and deter opportunistic thieves.

RFID-blocking compartments are specialized sections within bags or wallets that incorporate materials to shield radio frequency identification (RFID) signals. This feature is designed to protect sensitive information stored on RFID-enabled cards, such as credit cards and passports, from unauthorized scanning or electronic theft. The blocking technology helps prevent data skimming by creating a barrier that inhibits the transmission of RFID signals, enhancing the security of personal and financial information for individuals using these compartments.

2. Utilize Crossbody Bags

Crossbody bags are a style of bag that features a long strap, typically worn diagonally across the body, allowing the bag to rest at hip or waist level. The strap is designed to distribute the weight of the bag evenly, providing a comfortable and hands-free way to carry personal items.

Crossbody bags are not only stylish but also practical for deterring snatch theft. Worn across the body, they are harder for thieves to grab quickly compared to shoulder bags. Choose bags with secure closures and wear them close to your body.

3. Limit Visible Valuables

Minimize the display of expensive jewelry, gadgets, and other valuables in public. Thieves are often attracted to conspicuous targets, so keeping a low profile can reduce the likelihood of becoming a target.

4. Be Mindful of Your Surroundings

Situational awareness is a powerful tool in preventing snatch theft. Stay attentive to your surroundings, especially in crowded areas or places with a high incidence of theft. Avoid distractions such as excessive smartphone use, which can make you an easier target.

5. Secure Your Smartphone

Smartphones are a prime target for snatch thieves. Use a secure phone case with a strap, and consider installing tracking apps that can help locate your device in case it is stolen. Be cautious when using your phone in public spaces.

Conclusion

Snatch theft is a pervasive issue that requires a combination of preparedness, vigilance, and effective reactions. By staying calm in the face of a snatch attempt, prioritizing personal safety over possessions, and adopting proactive measures to secure belongings, individuals can significantly minimize the risk of falling victim to this type of quick theft.

While it's impossible to eliminate the threat entirely, a proactive mindset and practical strategies can empower individuals to navigate public spaces with confidence. Whether through the use of anti-theft bags, mindful awareness of surroundings, or strategic reactions to snatch attempts, everyone has the ability to contribute to their own safety and collectively create a more secure public environment.

Introduction

Kidnapping is a terrifying and unthinkable crime that can shatter lives and leave lasting scars on victims and their families. In recent times, the rise in incidents of abduction has heightened the need for individuals and families to be prepared and vigilant. This article explores essential strategies for kidnapping preparedness, emphasizing both adult personal safety and measures to protect children.

Understanding the Threat

Before delving into preparedness measures, it's crucial to understand the various motivations behind kidnappings. While some abductions are financially motivated, others may be driven by revenge, ideology, or personal vendettas. By recognizing the diversity of motives, individuals can tailor their preparedness plans to address specific risks.

Adult Personal Safety Tips

1. Situational Awareness

One of the most effective ways for adults to enhance their personal safety is by cultivating a heightened sense of situational awareness. This involves being mindful of one's surroundings, noticing unusual behavior, and staying alert to potential threats. Whether in a crowded market or a deserted parking lot, maintaining awareness can deter potential attackers.

2. Self-Defense Training

Engaging in self-defense training is an empowering step toward personal safety. Learning basic self-defense techniques can provide individuals with the skills and confidence needed to protect themselves in critical situations. Many communities offer self-defense classes tailored to various skill levels, making it accessible for everyone.

3. Communication Strategies

Effective communication can be a powerful tool in diffusing potentially dangerous situations. Individuals should practice assertiveness, clear communication, and the ability to set boundaries. This not only helps in everyday interactions but also enables people to communicate their discomfort or fear in situations where personal safety may be at risk.

4. Varying Daily Routines

Kidnappers often observe potential victims to understand their daily routines. Varying one's schedule can disrupt any surveillance and make it more challenging for a would-be kidnapper to predict patterns. This includes changing routes when walking or driving, altering gym schedules, and being unpredictable in daily activities.

5. Securing Personal Information

In the digital age, personal information is more accessible than ever. Adults should be cautious about sharing sensitive information online and ensure that their social media profiles are private. Cybersecurity measures should also be in place to prevent unauthorized access to personal data.

Child Safety Measures

1. Open Communication

Establishing open and honest communication with children is the foundation of any effective safety strategy. Parents should create an environment where children feel comfortable discussing their concerns and experiences. Encouraging open communication allows parents to address potential threats promptly.

2. Teaching Stranger Danger

Educating children about the concept of "stranger danger" is essential. Children should be taught to be cautious around unfamiliar individuals and to never accept gifts, rides, or invitations from strangers. Role-playing scenarios can help children practice appropriate responses to unfamiliar situations.

3. Establishing Safe Zones

Children should be familiar with safe zones in their environment. These can include designated meeting points, trusted neighbors' homes, or public spaces where they can seek help if they feel threatened. Reinforcing these safe zones provides children with a sense of security and a plan of action in case of an emergency.

4. Buddy System

A buddy system is a cooperative arrangement where individuals are paired or grouped together for mutual support, assistance, or safety. Encouraging the buddy system among children is a simple yet effective measure.

Whether walking to school or playing in the neighborhood, children are safer when they have a buddy. This system promotes mutual support and increases the chances of someone seeking help in case of an emergency.

5. Monitoring Online Activity

The online world poses unique threats to children. Parents should closely monitor their children's online activities, including social media interactions and gaming platforms. Educating children about the potential dangers of sharing personal information online is crucial for their safety.

Conclusion

In a world where threats to personal safety are ever-present, being prepared for the unthinkable is not a choice but a necessity. Kidnapping preparedness requires a combination of awareness, education, and proactive measures. By understanding the motivations behind kidnappings and implementing both adult personal safety tips and child safety measures, individuals and families can significantly reduce their vulnerability to abduction.

It is important to emphasize that preparedness is not about living in constant fear but about empowering oneself and loved ones with the tools and knowledge to navigate the world safely. Through a combination of awareness, communication, and practical strategies, we can strive to create a society where the risk of kidnapping is minimized, and everyone can live with a greater sense of security.

Introduction

In a world where safety concerns are paramount, sexual assault remains a pervasive issue that demands urgent attention. As we strive to create safer communities, it is crucial to empower individuals with the knowledge and skills needed to protect themselves. This article explores various strategies and approaches for sexual assault prevention, emphasizing the importance of education, awareness, and personal empowerment.

Understanding the Scope of the Issue

Sexual assault is a deeply troubling and prevalent crime that affects individuals of all ages, genders, and backgrounds. To effectively address this issue, it is essential to first understand its scope and impact on victims and communities. By acknowledging the prevalence of sexual assault, society can work towards creating a culture that rejects such behavior and actively promotes prevention.

Educating and Raising Awareness

Education is a powerful tool in the fight against sexual assault. Initiatives aimed at raising awareness about consent, healthy relationships, and the impact of sexual violence can contribute significantly to prevention. Schools, workplaces, and community organizations play a crucial role in fostering an environment where individuals are knowledgeable about their rights and responsibilities.

Teaching Consent and Boundaries

One key aspect of sexual assault prevention is promoting a clear understanding of consent and boundaries. Establishing open and honest conversations about consent, both within intimate relationships and in general social interactions, is vital. Educational programs should emphasize the importance of enthusiastic and ongoing consent, helping individuals recognize and respect personal boundaries.

Empowering Through Self-Defense Training

Empowering individuals with self-defense skills is a proactive approach to sexual assault prevention. Self-defense training not only provides practical tools for personal safety but also enhances confidence and assertiveness. By equipping individuals with the ability to protect themselves physically, we contribute to a culture that discourages potential perpetrators and promotes a sense of empowerment among potential victims.

Community Engagement and Support

Building strong communities that actively reject sexual violence is crucial for prevention. Encouraging community engagement and support networks creates an environment where individuals feel safe reporting incidents and seeking help. Community-led initiatives, such as neighborhood watch programs and support groups, contribute to a collective effort in safeguarding against sexual assault.

Challenging Stereotypes and Changing Cultural Norms

Sexual assault prevention requires challenging and changing deeply ingrained cultural norms and stereotypes.

Addressing toxic masculinity, dispelling myths about sexual violence, and promoting healthy attitudes towards sexuality are essential steps in creating a society that rejects and condemns sexual assault. Media, education, and public discourse play crucial roles in reshaping societal norms.

Utilizing Technology for Safety

In the digital age, technology can be harnessed for sexual assault prevention. Mobile apps, online platforms, and wearable devices can serve as tools for personal safety. From virtual support networks to real-time location sharing, technology offers innovative solutions that can be integrated into everyday life to enhance individual safety.

Workplace Policies and Training

Workplaces play a significant role in the lives of individuals, and implementing comprehensive sexual assault prevention policies is essential. Training employees on recognizing and addressing inappropriate behavior, creating a safe reporting environment, and fostering a culture of accountability are key components of workplace initiatives against sexual assault.

Government Initiatives and Legal Reforms

Governments have a critical role in addressing sexual assault through legal reforms and initiatives. Stricter laws, improved law enforcement training, and increased funding for victim support services are essential components of a comprehensive approach. Additionally, public awareness campaigns led by government agencies can contribute to changing attitudes and behaviors on a societal level.

Supporting Survivors and Breaking the Silence

Supporting survivors is an integral part of sexual assault prevention. Breaking the silence surrounding sexual violence encourages survivors to come forward, seek help, and report incidents. Creating a culture that believes and supports survivors not only helps them heal but also sends a powerful message that sexual assault will not be tolerated.

Conclusion

Sexual assault prevention requires a multifaceted approach that combines education, awareness, and empowerment. By fostering a culture that prioritizes consent, challenges harmful stereotypes, and utilizes technology for safety, we can create environments where individuals feel secure and protected. Community engagement, workplace initiatives, and government-led reforms are all vital components of a comprehensive strategy to safeguard against sexual assault. As we collectively strive for safer communities, it is imperative to empower individuals with the knowledge and tools they need to stay safe and contribute to a society that unequivocally rejects sexual violence.

Introduction

In the hustle and bustle of modern life, the roadways often serve as a microcosm of our daily stressors. As we navigate through traffic, the potential for encounters with aggressive behavior on the road, commonly known as road rage, looms large. This phenomenon is not only a threat to personal safety but also contributes to the overall deterioration of the driving experience. In this article, we will explore the dynamics of road rage, safe driving practices to avoid confrontations, and valuable tips for defusing road rage situations. By understanding and implementing these strategies, drivers can contribute to a safer and more harmonious driving environment.

Understanding Road Rage

Road rage is a complex and multifaceted issue that stems from a combination of individual temperament, external stressors, and the inherently frustrating nature of traffic. It manifests in various forms, ranging from aggressive tailgating and excessive speeding to verbal altercations and physical violence. Identifying the signs of road rage is crucial for both self-awareness and the ability to respond appropriately.

Safe Driving Practices to Avoid Confrontations

1. Maintain a Calm Demeanor

One of the most effective ways to prevent road rage incidents is to cultivate a calm and composed mindset while driving. Accept that traffic is an inevitable part of daily life and practice patience. Deep breaths and a positive attitude can go a long way in preventing the escalation of minor annoyances into full-blown confrontations.

2. Avoid Aggressive Driving Behaviors

Aggressive driving often begets more aggression. Refrain from tailgating, cutting off other drivers, or engaging in aggressive gestures. By driving defensively and avoiding confrontational behaviors, you reduce the likelihood of provoking others on the road.

3. Use Signals and Communicate Effectively

Clear communication on the road is key to avoiding misunderstandings that can lead to road rage. Use your turn signals, obey traffic rules, and make your intentions clear to other drivers. When changing lanes or merging, do so smoothly and predictably, giving those around you ample time to react.

4. Plan Ahead and Allow Extra Time

Many road rage incidents are triggered by the stress of being late. Plan your journeys with extra time to spare, reducing the pressure to speed or make aggressive maneuvers. By allowing for unexpected delays, you can approach your drive with a more relaxed mindset.

5. Practice Defensive Driving

Defensive driving involves anticipating the actions of other drivers and being prepared for unexpected situations. Stay aware of your surroundings, maintain a safe following distance, and be ready to react to the actions of other road users. By adopting a defensive driving mindset, you contribute to a safer road environment for everyone.

Tips for Defusing Road Rage Situations

1. Avoid Eye Contact and Ignore Provocations

If you find yourself the target of aggressive behavior, avoid making eye contact with the aggressor. Acknowledging their actions may escalate the situation. Instead, focus on driving safely and ignore provocative gestures or comments. Your goal is to de-escalate the tension and disengage from the conflict.

2. Stay Inside Your Vehicle

In the event of a confrontation, it's safest to remain inside your vehicle. Rolling down your window or stepping out can escalate the situation and put you at greater risk. Lock your doors, stay calm, and wait for the other driver to move on.

3. Report Aggressive Drivers

If you feel threatened by another driver's behavior, don't hesitate to contact the authorities. Provide a description of the vehicle, its license plate number, and details of the incident. Reporting aggressive drivers not only contributes to public safety but also helps law enforcement address potential issues before they escalate.

4. Find an Exit Route

If you find yourself in a situation where the aggression is escalating, look for an exit route. Change lanes or take an alternate route to distance yourself from the aggressor.

Prioritize your safety over any desire to confront or retaliate.

In the age of smartphones, documenting incidents can be a useful tool. If you feel threatened, discreetly use your phone to record the aggressive behavior. This can serve as valuable evidence if legal action becomes necessary, and it may also act as a deterrent for the aggressor.

Conclusion

Road rage is a societal challenge that requires a collective effort to address. By incorporating safe driving practices and adopting effective strategies for defusing road rage situations, drivers can contribute to a more harmonious and safer road environment. Cultivating a calm and patient mindset, avoiding aggressive behaviors, and knowing how to respond to aggression are all essential components of responsible and considerate driving. As we navigate the complex web of roadways, let us strive for understanding, empathy, and a shared commitment to making our roads safer for everyone.

Introduction

Responsible drinking is a crucial aspect of maintaining a healthy and balanced lifestyle. While enjoying alcoholic beverages is a common social activity, it is imperative to understand the potential consequences of excessive drinking, particularly when it leads to public intoxication. This article aims to shed light on the legal ramifications of public intoxication, the importance of alcohol awareness and moderation, and the overall significance of making responsible choices when consuming alcohol.

Legal Consequences of Public Intoxication

Public intoxication, often colloquially referred to as being "drunk and disorderly", is a legal offense in many jurisdictions. The severity of penalties may vary, but the common thread is that public intoxication is viewed as a threat to public safety. Law enforcement agencies take this matter seriously, as the behavior associated with intoxication can lead to disturbances, accidents, and even violence.

1. Criminal Charges and Fines

Public intoxication can result in criminal charges, leading to fines and legal consequences. The specifics vary by location, but individuals caught in a state of public drunkenness may find themselves facing fines, community service, or even short-term imprisonment. Such legal implications not only tarnish one's record but can also impact employment opportunities and future prospects.

2. Protecting Public Safety

The essence of laws against public intoxication lies in the protection of public safety. Intoxicated individuals are more prone to accidents, impaired judgment, and unpredictable behavior. By discouraging public intoxication, authorities aim to create a safer environment for everyone.

3. Impact on Driving Under the Influence (DUI) Charges

Public intoxication can be a precursor to more serious offenses, such as driving under the influence (DUI). Law enforcement officers often intervene when they suspect individuals are too impaired to operate a vehicle safely. Avoiding public intoxication is a crucial step in preventing DUI charges and the potential harm it poses to oneself and others.

Alcohol Awareness and Moderation

1. Understanding Personal Limits

Responsible drinking begins with understanding personal limits. Each individual metabolizes alcohol differently, and factors such as weight, age, and overall health play a role in how alcohol affects the body. Knowing one's limits is essential to avoid overconsumption and the associated risks.

2. Educating the Public

Promoting alcohol awareness is key to fostering responsible drinking habits. Educational campaigns, both in schools and communities, can provide information on the effects of alcohol, signs of intoxication, and the importance of moderation. By increasing public awareness, we empower individuals to make informed decisions regarding alcohol consumption.

3. Encouraging Responsible Serving Practices

Responsibility extends beyond the individual to establishments that serve alcohol. Bars, restaurants, and other venues must adhere to responsible serving practices, including checking identification, monitoring patrons' alcohol intake, and refusing service to visibly intoxicated individuals. By collectively adopting responsible practices, the entire community can contribute to a safer drinking culture.

4. Promoting Alternatives to Drinking

Responsible drinking involves recognizing when to abstain. Promoting alternatives to drinking, such as non-alcoholic beverages or engaging in activities that don't revolve around alcohol, can help create a more diverse and inclusive social scene. Encouraging social connections beyond the bar can contribute to a healthier and more balanced lifestyle.

Conclusion

Responsible drinking goes hand in hand with avoiding public intoxication and its consequences. Legal repercussions, ranging from fines to criminal charges, highlight the seriousness with which society views public intoxication. By understanding personal limits, promoting alcohol awareness, and encouraging responsible serving practices, we can collectively create an environment that values moderation and safety.

As individuals, we bear the responsibility of making informed choices about alcohol consumption, considering not only our own well-being but also the safety of those around us. Responsible drinking is not just a personal choice; it is a commitment to fostering a culture of moderation and mindfulness in our communities. By embracing these principles, we can contribute to a safer and more enjoyable social landscape for everyone.

Introduction

In the rapidly evolving landscape of the digital age, fraud has become an ever-present threat, with perpetrators employing increasingly sophisticated tactics to deceive individuals and organizations alike. As technology advances, so do the methods used by fraudsters, making it imperative for people to stay informed and vigilant. This article explores the importance of fraud awareness, strategies to safeguard personal and financial information, common scams to watch out for, and the necessity of a collective effort to combat fraudulent practices.

Safeguarding Personal and Financial Information

1. The Digital Age and Information Vulnerability

In an era dominated by technology, personal and financial information is more vulnerable than ever. From online shopping to social media interactions, every digital transaction leaves a trace. Understanding the risks associated with sharing information online is the first step toward safeguarding oneself from potential fraud.

2. Securing Personal Devices

With smartphones and computers playing an integral role in daily life, securing these devices is paramount. Utilizing strong passwords, enabling two-factor authentication, and keeping software up-to-date are essential practices to create a robust defense against potential breaches.

3. Phishing Attacks and Email Security

Phishing remains one of the most prevalent forms of online fraud. Fraudsters often disguise themselves as trustworthy entities to manipulate individuals into providing sensitive information. Recognizing phishing attempts, verifying sender identities, and refraining from clicking on suspicious links are fundamental precautions in the fight against phishing.

4. Social Engineering Tactics

Fraudsters exploit human psychology through social engineering tactics. This involves manipulating individuals into divulging confidential information or performing actions that may compromise their security. Being aware of common social engineering techniques, such as impersonation and pretexting, empowers individuals to recognize and resist these deceptive practices. Pretexting is a deceptive practice in which an individual fabricates a false scenario or pretext to manipulate others into divulging sensitive information or performing actions they might not otherwise do.

5. Public Wi-Fi Risks

Public Wi-Fi networks pose a significant risk to personal information security. These networks are often less secure, making it easier for hackers to intercept data. Avoiding sensitive transactions on public Wi-Fi and using virtual private networks (VPNs) are effective measures to mitigate this risk.

Identifying Common Scams

1. Online Shopping Scams

The rise of e-commerce has brought convenience, but it has also given rise to online shopping scams. Fake websites, counterfeit products, and deceptive payment methods are some tactics employed by fraudsters. Verifying the legitimacy of websites, reading reviews, and using secure payment methods are crucial steps in avoiding online shopping scams.

2. Tech Support Scams

Tech support scams involve fraudsters posing as legitimate technical support representatives. They often contact individuals claiming that their devices are infected with malware or viruses. Recognizing the signs of a tech support scam, such as unsolicited calls or pop-up messages, is vital for preventing falling victim to these deceptive practices.

3. Phony Investment Schemes

Investment fraud is a persistent threat, with scammers enticing individuals with promises of high returns. Recognizing the red flags of investment scams, such as guaranteed profits and pressure tactics, is essential for protecting one's financial assets.

4. Romance Scams

With the increasing popularity of online dating, romance scams have become prevalent. Fraudsters create fake profiles to establish romantic relationships and then exploit emotions to extort money. Exercising caution, verifying identities, and refraining from sending money to strangers online are critical in avoiding romance scams.

5. Government Impersonation Scams

Scammers often impersonate government officials, law enforcement officers, or tax authorities to instill fear and manipulate individuals into providing personal information or payments. Understanding that government agencies rarely contact individuals through unsolicited calls and verifying the legitimacy of such communications can help thwart government impersonation scams.

Conclusion

In the digital age, fraud awareness is not just a personal responsibility but a collective necessity. The evolving tactics of fraudsters require a proactive approach from individuals, businesses, and regulatory bodies. Safeguarding personal and financial information demands a combination of technological measures, such as secure passwords and encryption, along with a heightened awareness of common scams and deceptive practices.

Recognizing the signs of fraud is paramount to avoiding falling victim to scams. Whether it's phishing attempts, online shopping fraud, or investment schemes, individuals must remain vigilant and educate themselves on the evolving tactics employed by fraudsters. By understanding the risks associated with various online activities and adopting proactive security measures, individuals can significantly reduce their susceptibility to fraud.

In conclusion, the fight against fraud is a shared responsibility that necessitates a collaborative effort from individuals, businesses, and law enforcement. By staying informed, implementing best practices for personal and financial security, and reporting suspicious activities, we can collectively create a safer digital environment. As technology continues to advance, so must our awareness and resilience against deceptive practices to ensure a secure and trustworthy online ecosystem.

Introduction

In an era dominated by digital interactions, the safeguarding of our personal information has become a paramount concern. Identity theft, a malicious act that involves the unauthorized use of someone's personal information for financial gain or other fraudulent activities, has surged with the increasing prevalence of online transactions and communication. As we navigate the digital landscape, it becomes imperative to fortify our defenses against identity theft and protect our digital persona. This article explores key aspects of identity theft protection, from recognizing phishing attempts to adopting secure password practices.

Recognizing Phishing Attempts

Phishing, a deceptive practice where cybercriminals attempt to acquire sensitive information by posing as trustworthy entities, remains a prevalent threat in the digital realm. Recognizing phishing attempts is the first line of defense against identity theft.

1. Email Awareness

Phishing often takes the form of deceptive emails, where attackers impersonate legitimate organizations. Be vigilant about unsolicited emails, especially those urging immediate action or claiming urgency. Legitimate organizations usually communicate through secure channels and avoid requesting sensitive information via email.

2. Check URLs

Phishers often create fake websites that mimic legitimate ones. Before clicking on any links, hover over them to inspect the URL. Legitimate websites use secure connections (https://), and discrepancies in the URL structure can signal a phishing attempt.

3. Be Skeptical of Attachments

Phishing emails may contain malicious attachments designed to install malware on your device. Avoid opening attachments from unknown sources, and verify the sender's identity before downloading any files.

4. Verify Communication Requests

Cybercriminals may attempt to exploit trust by posing as colleagues, friends, or family members. Always verify unexpected communication requests, especially those seeking personal or financial information.

Secure Password Practices

Passwords are the gatekeepers to our digital identities. Adopting secure password practices is crucial to thwarting identity theft attempts and enhancing overall cybersecurity.

1. Complexity is Key

Create strong passwords that combine uppercase and lowercase letters, numbers, and special characters. Avoid easily guessable information like birthdays or names, and refrain from using the same password across multiple accounts.

2. Password Managers

Implementing a password manager can simplify the process of managing complex passwords for multiple accounts. Password managers generate and store strong, unique passwords for each account, reducing the risk of a security breach if one password is compromised.

3. Two-Factor Authentication (2FA)

Enable 2FA whenever possible. This additional layer of security requires users to provide a second form of verification, such as a code sent to a mobile device, in addition to their password. Even if a password is compromised, 2FA adds an extra barrier.

4. Regular Updates

Change passwords regularly, especially after any security incident or data breach. Regular updates help mitigate the risk of unauthorized access, as compromised passwords lose their efficacy over time.

Conclusion

As we traverse the intricate web of the digital world, the onus lies on us to fortify our defenses against identity theft. Recognizing phishing attempts and adopting secure password practices are pivotal steps in safeguarding our digital persona. The evolving landscape of cyber threats requires continuous vigilance and adaptation to emerging security measures.

By staying informed and implementing best practices, individuals can significantly reduce their vulnerability to identity theft. Awareness is the cornerstone of effective protection, and as technology advances, so must our understanding of the risks involved. As we move forward in this digital age, let us empower ourselves with the knowledge and tools necessary to navigate the online landscape securely.

In conclusion, the responsibility for protecting our digital identities rests with each of us. Through a combination of awareness, vigilance, and proactive security measures, we can create a robust defense against identity theft and ensure a safer and more secure digital future.

Introduction

In a world where personal security is paramount, safeguarding our personal belongings has become a crucial aspect of daily life. The increasing prevalence of theft in various forms necessitates a proactive approach to protecting our possessions. Whether it's safeguarding items in public spaces or fortifying the security of our homes, adopting effective strategies is essential. This article explores comprehensive approaches to prevent theft and ensure the safety of personal property.

Safeguarding Personal Belongings in Public Spaces

Public spaces can be a breeding ground for opportunistic theft, making it imperative for individuals to be vigilant and adopt protective strategies.

1. Mindful Awareness

One of the first steps in protecting personal property in public spaces is cultivating mindful awareness. This involves staying attentive to your surroundings, being conscious of your belongings, and avoiding unnecessary distractions. Criminals often seize the opportunity when individuals are engrossed in their smartphones or engaged in other activities, making them easy targets. By staying alert, you can significantly reduce the risk of theft.

2. Secure Bags and Pockets

Practical measures such as securing bags and pockets can act as deterrents for potential thieves. Use bags with zippers or secure closures and keep them close to your body. Avoid leaving valuables in easily accessible pockets, and instead, opt for inside pockets or money belts for essential items. A money belt is a discreet and wearable pouch designed to securely hold and conceal valuables, such as cash, credit cards, and passports, providing a practical solution for travelers to safeguard their belongings while on the move. Additionally, backpacks should be worn on both shoulders to make them more challenging for opportunistic thieves to grab.

3. Utilize Anti-Theft Devices

Innovative anti-theft devices are increasingly available to enhance the security of personal belongings. These may include RFID-blocking wallets to protect against electronic theft, as well as GPS tracking devices that can help locate lost or stolen items. RFID-blocking wallets are specially designed wallets that contain materials to shield against radio frequency identification (RFID) signals. These wallets are intended to protect contactless cards, passports, and other RFID-enabled items from unauthorized scanning or skimming, enhancing the security of personal information and preventing potential identity theft or fraud. Investing in such technology can add an extra layer of protection and peace of mind.

4. Travel Safes and Locks

When traveling or spending time in crowded areas, consider using travel safes or locks to secure valuable items. Portable safes with combination locks provide a secure place to store passports, jewelry, and other valuables in hotel rooms or temporary accommodations. Similarly, luggage locks can prevent unauthorized access to your belongings during transit.

5. Be Cautious with Public Wi-Fi

In an era of constant connectivity, the use of public Wi-Fi is widespread. However, it's crucial to exercise caution when accessing personal accounts or conducting financial transactions in public spaces. Public Wi-Fi networks can be vulnerable to hacking, putting your sensitive information at risk. Using a virtual private network (VPN) adds an extra layer of security by encrypting your internet connection, making it more challenging for cybercriminals to intercept data.

Home Security Measures

While protecting personal belongings in public spaces is essential, securing our homes is equally crucial. Implementing robust home security measures can deter potential thieves and provide a sense of safety within our private spaces.

1. Install Quality Locks

The foundation of home security lies in the strength and reliability of your locks. Install high-quality deadbolt locks on all exterior doors, including garage doors. Reinforce door frames to prevent forced entry, and consider upgrading to smart locks that offer advanced features such as remote monitoring and keyless entry.

2. Adequate Lighting

Well-lit homes create an environment that is less conducive to theft. Ensure that the exterior of your home, including entry points and pathways, is well-lit. Motion-activated lights are an effective deterrent, as they surprise potential intruders and draw attention to suspicious activity.

3. Window Security

Windows are common points of entry for burglars, so it's essential to fortify them. Install window locks, reinforce glass with security film, and consider adding window bars or grilles for additional protection. Be mindful of open or partially open windows, especially on lower floors, as they can be exploited by intruders.

4. Home Security Systems

Investing in a comprehensive home security system provides a proactive defense against theft. Modern systems include features such as surveillance cameras, motion detectors, and alarm systems. Visible security cameras act as a deterrent, while monitored alarm systems can alert authorities in the event of a break-in.

5. Safe Storage

For valuable items such as jewelry, important documents, or cash, consider using a home safe. Choose a safe that is both secure and fire-resistant. Safes can be anchored to the floor or wall, making them more challenging for thieves to remove. This ensures that even if an intruder gains access to your home, certain valuables remain protected.

Conclusion

Protecting personal property requires a multifaceted approach that encompasses both public spaces and the home environment. By adopting strategies such as mindful awareness, secure storage, and advanced security measures, individuals can significantly reduce the risk of theft and enhance overall safety. Whether on the go or within the comfort of our homes, prioritizing the protection of personal belongings contributes to a more secure and resilient lifestyle.

Introduction

In a world where personal safety is a growing concern, the need for proactive measures to reduce homicide risks has become increasingly apparent. Homicide, the unlawful killing of one person by another, is a tragic and complex issue that affects individuals, families, and communities. This article explores the multifaceted approach to reducing homicide risks, focusing on personal security enhancement through community initiatives, safety planning, and broader societal engagement.

Community Initiatives for Violence Prevention

1. Community Policing and Engagement

One of the cornerstones of reducing homicide risks lies in fostering strong relationships between law enforcement agencies and the communities they serve. Community policing strategies emphasize collaboration, communication, and trust-building. Officers working closely with residents can address concerns, identify potential risks, and implement preventative measures.

2. Youth Outreach and Mentorship Programs

Investing in the youth is critical for breaking the cycle of violence. Community initiatives that provide mentorship, education, and positive outlets for young people can steer them away from potential life paths that may involve crime. By addressing the root causes of violence, communities can create a safer environment for everyone.

3. Anti-Gang Initiatives

Gang-related violence is a significant contributor to homicide rates in many communities. Implementing anti-gang initiatives that focus on prevention, intervention, and rehabilitation can disrupt the cycle of gang violence. Outreach programs offering alternatives to gang involvement, coupled with law enforcement efforts, can contribute to a safer community.

4. Public Awareness Campaigns

Raising awareness about the consequences of violence and promoting conflict resolution skills is essential. Public campaigns can educate individuals on recognizing and addressing signs of aggression, providing resources for conflict resolution, and fostering a culture of non-violence within the community.

Personal Safety Planning

1. Risk Assessment

Personal safety planning begins with a thorough risk assessment. Individuals should evaluate their daily routines, identify potential risks, and assess vulnerabilities. This process involves considering factors such as location, time of day, and personal habits that may inadvertently expose someone to danger.

2. Self-Defense Training

Empowering individuals with the skills to protect themselves is a fundamental aspect of personal safety planning. Self-defense training equips individuals with techniques to neutralize threats and escape potentially dangerous situations. These skills not only enhance personal safety but also contribute to an overall sense of empowerment.

3. Technology and Personal Safety Apps

In the digital age, technology plays a crucial role in personal safety. Various apps and devices offer features such as location tracking, emergency alerts, and virtual companion services. Integrating technology into personal safety planning provides an additional layer of security and facilitates quick response in times of crisis.

4. Home Security Measures

Home is often considered a sanctuary, but it can also be a target for violence. Implementing effective home security measures, such as robust locks, surveillance systems, and well-lit exteriors, can significantly reduce the risk of home-related incidents. Educating individuals on these measures ensures a safer living environment.

Conclusion

In the pursuit of reducing homicide risks, a comprehensive strategy that combines community initiatives and personal safety planning is paramount. Community engagement, through initiatives like community policing, mentorship programs, and anti-gang efforts, addresses the societal roots of violence. Simultaneously, personal safety planning empowers individuals to take charge of their own security.

Efforts to reduce homicide risks should not be isolated; rather, they should be part of a broader societal commitment to fostering a culture of safety and well-being.

Public awareness campaigns play a crucial role in educating communities about the impact of violence and promoting peaceful conflict resolution.

As we navigate an ever-changing world, the synergy between community-driven initiatives and individual responsibility forms a robust framework for reducing homicide risks. By fostering collaboration, implementing preventative measures, and empowering individuals with the tools they need, we can strive towards safer communities where the threat of homicide is significantly diminished.

Introduction

Drug trafficking refers to the illegal trade and distribution of controlled substances, such as narcotics, across national or regional borders. It involves the production, transportation, and sale of illicit drugs, often organized by criminal enterprises. Governments and law enforcement agencies globally work to combat drug trafficking through international cooperation, border controls, intelligence sharing, and targeted law enforcement operations to disrupt and dismantle drug cartels and networks. The fight against drug trafficking aims to reduce the availability of illegal drugs, curb related criminal activities, and address the associated public health and social consequences.

Drug trafficking is a pervasive issue that plagues societies globally, causing immense harm to individuals and communities. The battle against this illicit trade requires a multi-faceted approach, with one crucial aspect being the recognition and reporting of suspicious activities. This article explores the importance of community involvement, the role of education in preventing youth involvement in drug-related activities, and the significance of reporting suspicious behavior to curb the menace of drug trafficking.

Educating Youth about the Dangers of Drug Involvement

A cornerstone in the fight against drug trafficking is education, particularly aimed at the youth. Young individuals are often susceptible to the allure of drugs due to various factors such as peer pressure, curiosity, or a desire to escape from challenges they may be facing. Thus, a proactive approach involves instilling awareness about the dangers and consequences of drug involvement.

Educational institutions play a pivotal role in this endeavor. Incorporating comprehensive drug education into school curricula ensures that students are equipped with the knowledge necessary to make informed decisions. Beyond classroom settings, community outreach programs and partnerships with local organizations can supplement formal education, providing a more holistic understanding of the ramifications of drug use.

It is crucial to convey not only the physical risks associated with drug abuse but also the broader societal implications. Drug trafficking fuels crime, violence, and instability within communities. By emphasizing these aspects, educators can instill a sense of responsibility in young minds, fostering a generation that actively opposes drug-related activities.

Community Involvement in Drug Prevention

A resilient defense against drug trafficking requires the active engagement of communities. Local residents are the first line of defense in identifying and reporting suspicious activities that may be indicative of drug trafficking. Establishing a strong sense of community and promoting a culture of vigilance can significantly contribute to deterring illicit drug operations.

Neighborhood watch programs are effective tools in mobilizing communities against drug trafficking. These programs encourage residents to be vigilant, observe their surroundings, and report any unusual activities to law enforcement. Building trust and open communication between community members and law enforcement agencies is pivotal, as it fosters a collaborative environment that is essential for combating drug-related crimes.

Community leaders, including religious figures, educators, and local authorities, play a crucial role in galvanizing collective efforts. They can organize awareness campaigns, workshops, and town hall meetings to educate residents about the signs of drug trafficking and the importance of reporting suspicious activities promptly. Creating a network of support within the community ensures that individuals feel empowered to take action against drug-related issues.

Furthermore, engaging with at-risk populations within the community is essential. Establishing rehabilitation and support programs for individuals struggling with substance abuse can address the root causes of drug-related problems. By offering alternatives and support systems, communities can contribute to breaking the cycle of addiction and preventing vulnerable individuals from becoming entangled in the web of drug trafficking.

Recognizing and Reporting Suspicious Activity

Recognizing and reporting suspicious activities is a critical component of the community's role in combating drug trafficking. Law enforcement agencies rely on the eyes and ears of the public to gather valuable information that may lead to the dismantling of drug networks. Understanding what constitutes suspicious behavior is essential for community members to actively contribute to this effort.

Unusual patterns of behavior, unexplained financial transactions, and frequent visitors at odd hours can be indicators of potential drug-related activities. Additionally, the presence of certain paraphernalia, such as large quantities of cash, weapons, or chemicals, may signal illicit operations. Training community members to recognize these signs empowers them to act as proactive agents in the fight against drug trafficking.

Anonymity and protection for those who report suspicious activities are crucial components of an effective reporting system. Community members need assurance that their cooperation will not jeopardize their safety. Establishing confidential reporting mechanisms, such as hotlines or online platforms, encourages individuals to come forward without fear of reprisal.

Law enforcement agencies, in turn, must actively engage with the community to create a feedback loop. Providing updates on the outcomes of reported incidents fosters trust and reinforces the idea that community involvement is integral to successfully combating drug trafficking. Recognizing the efforts of individuals who play a role in reporting and preventing drug-related activities can further motivate community members to remain vigilant.

Conclusion

In the relentless battle against drug trafficking, recognizing and reporting suspicious activities emerges as a powerful weapon at the community's disposal. Education, particularly targeted at the youth, forms the foundation for preventing drug involvement and cultivating a generation that is resilient against the allure of illicit substances. Community involvement amplifies the impact of these educational efforts, creating a united front against drug trafficking.

As communities become proactive in identifying and reporting suspicious behavior, they contribute significantly to the broader efforts of law enforcement agencies. Recognizing the signs of drug-related activities and promptly reporting them is not only a civic duty but a collective responsibility that can safeguard neighborhoods and promote the well-being of society as a whole. Through education, community engagement, and a commitment to reporting, we can create a future where the grip of drug trafficking is loosened, allowing communities to thrive in safety and prosperity.

Introduction

In an era where the sanctity of our homes is constantly challenged, the need for robust home security has become paramount. The concept of home security extends beyond the installation of locks and alarms; it involves a holistic approach that encompasses risk assessment, strategic planning, and community involvement. In this article, we delve into the multifaceted realm of home security, exploring burglary prevention, the role of technology in home security systems, and the significance of community initiatives like neighborhood watch programs.

Burglary Prevention

1. Risk Assessment and Vulnerability Analysis

Before implementing any security measures, a comprehensive risk assessment is crucial. Identifying vulnerabilities in and around your home allows for a targeted and effective security strategy. Factors such as location, neighborhood crime rates, and your daily routines contribute to this analysis. Professionals can assist in evaluating potential weaknesses, helping you prioritize security enhancements.

2. Home Security Systems

Modern technology has revolutionized home security with the advent of sophisticated systems. From basic alarm systems to advanced smart home security, options abound. A central monitoring system that integrates surveillance cameras, motion detectors, and door/window sensors provides real-time information and alerts. Smart home security allows remote monitoring and control via mobile devices, offering an unprecedented level of convenience and peace of mind.

3. Securing Doors and Windows

Doors and windows are primary entry points for burglars. Reinforcing these access points is fundamental to home security. Solid doors with quality deadbolt locks, strike plates, and peepholes offer a sturdy first line of defense. Windows can be fortified with laminated glass or security film, deterring break-ins. For added protection, consider installing window locks and reinforcing frames.

4. Outdoor Lighting

Adequate outdoor lighting is an essential but often overlooked aspect of home security. Well-lit exteriors discourage trespassers and provide a clear view of the surroundings. Motion-activated lights near entry points and along pathways are effective in deterring intruders. Strategic placement of lighting fixtures contributes to a sense of security and can be a cost-effective addition to your overall security plan.

5. Landscaping for Security

Landscaping can be a double-edged sword in home security. While a well-maintained yard enhances curb appeal, overgrown bushes and trees can serve as hiding spots for criminals. Prune vegetation near windows and eliminate potential hiding spots. Additionally, consider planting thorny shrubs as a natural deterrent. The goal is to strike a balance between aesthetics and security, creating a welcoming but secure environment.

Community involvement is a powerful tool in combating crime. Neighborhood watch programs bring residents together, fostering a sense of unity and shared responsibility. Regular meetings and communication channels allow for the exchange of information and the swift reporting of suspicious activities. Collaborative efforts between neighbors and local law enforcement create a network that reinforces the overall safety of the community.

Conclusion

As we navigate the complexities of the modern world, ensuring the security of our homes is a responsibility that cannot be understated. Burglary prevention requires a proactive and multifaceted approach that encompasses risk assessment, advanced technology, and community engagement. By fortifying our doors and windows, embracing outdoor lighting, and participating in neighborhood watch programs, we create layers of defense that deter potential intruders. Home security is not just about protecting property; it's about safeguarding the sanctity and well-being of our families. In this dynamic landscape, staying one step ahead ensures that our homes remain the secure havens they are meant to be.

Introduction

In the intricate tapestry of parenting, ensuring the safety of our children stands as an unwavering priority. As children and teens navigate the world, the need to impart essential life skills, including personal safety, becomes paramount. This article delves into the multifaceted realm of personal safety, exploring key aspects such as stranger danger awareness, online safety, social media consciousness, and the crucial role of setting boundaries and effective communication.

Teaching Children about Stranger Danger

In the early stages of a child's life, the concept of "stranger danger" emerges as a fundamental lesson. Educating children about the potential risks associated with interacting with unfamiliar individuals lays the groundwork for a safety-conscious mindset. Parents and guardians play a pivotal role in imparting these lessons, emphasizing the importance of not engaging in conversations or accepting anything from strangers.

Stranger Danger Awareness

Stranger danger awareness extends beyond the simple avoidance of unfamiliar faces. It involves instilling a sense of discernment in children, empowering them to recognize situations that may pose a threat. Teaching children to trust their instincts and fostering open communication channels is essential. Encouraging them to identify safe spaces, such as trusted adults or public places, can further enhance their ability to navigate potentially risky situations.

Online Safety for Children

In today's digital age, the online realm presents both opportunities and challenges for children and teens. Parents and caregivers must actively engage in educating the younger generation about the importance of online safety. This includes understanding the potential risks associated with sharing personal information, recognizing and avoiding cyberbullying, and comprehending the consequences of engaging in inappropriate online behavior.

Social Media Awareness

The advent of social media has transformed the way children and teens communicate and connect with the world. Social media platforms offer opportunities for self-expression and community building, but they also expose users to potential dangers. Parents should engage in ongoing conversations about responsible social media use, emphasizing the significance of privacy settings, the potential consequences of oversharing, and the importance of reporting any suspicious or harmful online activities.

Setting Boundaries and Communication

Effective communication within the family unit serves as a cornerstone for personal safety. Parents and guardians must establish open and non-judgmental communication channels, creating an environment where children feel comfortable sharing their experiences and concerns. Setting clear boundaries regarding acceptable behaviors, both online and offline, helps children understand the parameters of safe and responsible conduct.

Moreover, fostering a sense of agency in children allows them to actively participate in decision-making processes related to their safety. Encouraging them to voice their opinions and preferences builds confidence and reinforces the idea that personal safety is a collaborative effort between parents and children.

School and Community Involvement

The responsibility of instilling personal safety values extends beyond the home. Schools and communities play integral roles in reinforcing these lessons and creating environments that prioritize the well-being of children and teens. Educational institutions should implement comprehensive safety programs that address various aspects, including stranger danger, online safety, and the potential risks associated with external influences.

Community involvement further fortifies the safety net around children. Collaboration between parents, schools, law enforcement, and community organizations enhances the collective effort to create safe spaces for children to grow and thrive. Neighborhood watch programs, workshops, and community events focused on personal safety contribute to a culture of vigilance and support.

Conclusion

In the intricate tapestry of personal safety for children and teens, a holistic approach is paramount. From the foundational lessons of stranger danger to the complexities of online safety and social media awareness, parents, caregivers, schools, and communities must work collaboratively to create an environment where children can flourish without compromising their well-being.

By instilling a sense of discernment, setting clear boundaries, and fostering open communication, we empower the younger generation to navigate the world with confidence and resilience. In the evolving landscape of personal safety, the collective efforts of families, schools, and communities serve as the threads that weave a protective shield around our children and teens, ensuring they embark on their journey with the tools and knowledge needed to thrive safely in the world.

Introduction

In the fast-paced and dynamic landscape of modern workplaces, ensuring the safety and well-being of employees has become paramount. Workplace safety goes beyond merely adhering to regulations; it involves creating a culture that prioritizes the health and security of every individual within the organization. This article explores various aspects of workplace safety, from emergency preparedness to mental health support, offering a comprehensive guide to fostering a secure and healthy work environment.

Strategies for a Secure and Healthy Work Environment

1. Emergency Preparedness

Emergencies can strike at any moment, ranging from natural disasters to accidents within the workplace. Establishing robust emergency preparedness protocols is crucial to mitigate potential risks and ensure the safety of employees. This involves conducting regular drills, implementing evacuation plans, and providing adequate training on emergency procedures. A well-prepared workforce is better equipped to handle unexpected situations, minimizing the impact on both individuals and the organization.

Conducting regular drills involves organized and simulated exercises designed to practice and assess the preparedness, response, and efficiency of individuals or groups in specific situations. These drills are common in various contexts, including emergency preparedness, workplace safety, schools, and military training. Regular drills help familiarize participants with procedures, identify areas for improvement, and ensure a prompt and effective response in real-life scenarios. Whether it's fire drills in schools or emergency evacuation drills in workplaces, the goal is to enhance overall safety and readiness through repetitive and realistic training exercises.

2. Health and Safety Policies

Clear and comprehensive health and safety policies form the backbone of a secure work environment. These policies should encompass a wide range of factors, including guidelines for handling hazardous materials, protocols for using machinery, and procedures for reporting safety concerns. Regular updates and communication regarding these policies are essential to keep employees informed and engaged in maintaining a safe workplace.

3. Workplace Violence Prevention

Workplace violence is an unfortunate reality that organizations must address. Prevention starts with fostering a culture of respect and open communication. Implementing security measures, such as access controls and surveillance systems, can act as deterrents. Additionally, providing training on conflict resolution and recognizing early signs of potential violence is crucial for creating a safe and supportive workplace.

4. Ergonomics and Physical Health

Physical health is closely tied to workplace safety. Poor ergonomics can lead to long-term health issues and decreased productivity. Employers should invest in ergonomic workspaces, providing comfortable furniture and equipment that reduces the risk of musculoskeletal disorders (conditions affecting the muscles, bones, tendons, ligaments, and other parts of the musculoskeletal system, often causing pain, stiffness, and impaired physical function). Regular breaks and exercises can also contribute to maintaining physical well-being, ensuring employees can perform their tasks safely and efficiently.

5. Mental Health Support

Acknowledging and addressing mental health in the workplace is as vital as physical health. High levels of stress and burnout can impact employee well-being and overall productivity. Organizations should promote a stigma-free environment where employees feel comfortable discussing mental health concerns. Providing access to counseling services, stress management programs, and promoting work-life balance can significantly contribute to a mentally healthy workplace.

6. Cybersecurity in the Workplace

In the digital age, cybersecurity is an integral component of workplace safety. As organizations rely on technology for day-to-day operations, protecting sensitive information becomes paramount. Implementing robust cybersecurity measures, such as firewalls, encryption, and regular security training for employees, safeguards against data breaches and cyber threats. A secure digital infrastructure is essential for maintaining the overall safety and integrity of the workplace.

Conclusion

Workplace safety is a multifaceted endeavor that requires a holistic approach. From emergency preparedness to mental health support, each aspect plays a crucial role in creating a secure and healthy work environment. Organizations that prioritize the well-being of their employees not only comply with regulations but also foster a positive culture that enhances productivity and employee satisfaction. By implementing the strategies discussed in this article, businesses can pave the way for a safer, healthier, and more successful future.

Introduction

Public order is the cornerstone of a thriving and peaceful society. It involves maintaining harmony and ensuring the safety of individuals within a community. In the quest for a well-functioning society, the emphasis is often placed on law enforcement. However, a more nuanced and effective approach involves fostering responsible behavior among the public. This article delves into the multifaceted aspects of maintaining public order, highlighting the importance of community policing initiatives, effective conflict resolution in public spaces, and the overall promotion of responsible behavior.

Community Policing Initiatives

Community policing is a philosophy that advocates for a collaborative approach between law enforcement agencies and the communities they serve. It seeks to build trust and partnerships, with the ultimate goal of enhancing public safety. One of the key aspects of community policing is the active involvement of police officers in community activities and events. This helps in breaking down the barriers between law enforcement and the public, fostering a sense of mutual understanding.

In practice, community policing involves officers working closely with community members to identify and address specific issues affecting public order. This can range from organizing neighborhood watch programs to conducting educational workshops on crime prevention. By engaging with the community proactively, law enforcement not only gains valuable insights into local concerns but also establishes a rapport that is essential for effective policing.

Furthermore, community policing emphasizes problem-solving rather than merely reacting to incidents. Police officers work alongside community members to identify root causes of problems and develop strategies to address them. This collaborative approach not only prevents crime but also promotes responsible behavior by encouraging individuals to take an active role in the safety and well-being of their community.

Conflict Resolution in Public Spaces

Conflicts are inevitable in any community, but how they are managed can significantly impact public order. Effective conflict resolution is crucial for maintaining harmony in public spaces. One approach involves empowering community members with conflict resolution skills, allowing them to address disputes before they escalate into more significant problems.

Educational programs and workshops that focus on communication, empathy, and mediation can be instrumental in equipping individuals with the tools necessary to resolve conflicts peacefully. By fostering a culture of dialogue and understanding, communities can create an environment where disputes are resolved amicably, reducing the strain on law enforcement resources.

Additionally, public spaces such as parks, streets, and communal areas often serve as the backdrop for conflicts. Designing these spaces with an emphasis on promoting positive interactions can contribute to reducing the likelihood of disputes. Well-lit areas, clear signage, and the strategic placement of community resources can create an environment that encourages responsible behavior and discourages antisocial activities.

Law enforcement agencies also play a pivotal role in conflict resolution. Officers trained in de-escalation techniques can defuse tense situations and prevent them from spiraling out of control. By prioritizing communication and understanding, officers can build trust with the public and contribute to a more peaceful coexistence.

Promoting Responsible Behavior

Promoting responsible behavior goes beyond law enforcement and community policing initiatives. It involves instilling a sense of civic responsibility in individuals, encouraging them to be active contributors to the well-being of their community. Educational programs that focus on citizenship, ethics, and social responsibility can be integrated into school curricula, ensuring that future generations understand the importance of responsible behavior.

Moreover, community leaders, including religious figures, educators, and influencers, can play a pivotal role in shaping public attitudes. Their influence extends beyond formal institutions, and by leveraging their standing in the community, they can promote values that contribute to a more responsible and orderly society.

Public awareness campaigns are another effective tool for promoting responsible behavior. These campaigns can address specific issues such as littering, vandalism, or substance abuse, fostering a collective sense of responsibility for the community's well-being. By highlighting the impact of individual actions on the broader community, these campaigns seek to create a culture of accountability.

Conclusion

Maintaining public order requires a holistic and collaborative approach that extends beyond traditional law enforcement measures. Community policing initiatives, effective conflict resolution strategies, and the promotion of responsible behavior are integral components of a comprehensive framework for a peaceful society.

Community policing builds bridges between law enforcement and the public, fostering collaboration and trust. Conflict resolution techniques empower individuals to address disputes peacefully, reducing the strain on law enforcement resources. Promoting responsible behavior involves a combination of education, community engagement, and public awareness campaigns to instill a sense of civic duty.

By adopting these approaches, communities can create environments where responsible behavior is the norm, contributing to a safer and more harmonious society. As we navigate the complexities of modern living, the emphasis on these proactive measures becomes increasingly crucial in building resilient and cohesive communities.

Introduction

In the age of rapid technological advancement, our reliance on digital platforms has grown exponentially. From personal communication to business operations, the digital landscape has become an integral part of our daily lives. However, this increased connectivity also brings about heightened risks, with hackers and cybercriminals exploiting vulnerabilities for malicious purposes. In this article, we will explore the critical aspects of securing digital spaces and protecting against hacking.

Identifying and Reporting Cyber Threats

1. Understanding the Threat Landscape

Before delving into the specifics of cybersecurity, it's crucial to comprehend the diverse landscape of cyber threats. Hackers employ various techniques, including malware, phishing, ransomware, and more, to exploit weaknesses in digital systems. Recognizing the multifaceted nature of these threats is the first step toward building a robust defense.

2. The Role of Vigilance and Awareness

Creating a secure digital environment starts with cultivating a culture of vigilance and awareness among users. Regular cybersecurity training and awareness programs can empower individuals to recognize potential threats. Users should be educated on the latest hacking tactics, phishing schemes, and social engineering techniques to bolster their ability to identify and report suspicious activities.

3. Incident Response and Reporting Protocols

Establishing clear incident response and reporting protocols is fundamental in minimizing the impact of a cyber attack. Organizations should have well-defined procedures for reporting suspicious activities promptly. This includes creating channels for reporting incidents, implementing a structured incident response plan, and designating responsible individuals or teams to handle security breaches.

4. Collaboration with Cybersecurity Authorities

In the event of a cyber attack, collaboration with cybersecurity authorities is essential. Governments and law enforcement agencies often have dedicated units to handle cybercrime. Organizations should establish partnerships with these entities to facilitate the swift response and investigation of cyber incidents. Reporting incidents promptly not only helps in mitigating the immediate impact but also contributes to the collective efforts in combating cybercrime.

Cybersecurity Best Practices

1. Implementing Strong Access Controls

One of the primary methods to thwart hacking attempts is the implementation of robust access controls. Limiting access to sensitive data and systems ensures that only authorized individuals can interact with critical assets. This involves using strong authentication methods, such as multi-factor authentication (MFA), and regularly reviewing and updating user access privileges.

2. Regular Software Updates and Patch Management

Outdated software and unpatched systems are often exploited by hackers. Regularly updating software and implementing effective patch management strategies are crucial for closing potential security loopholes. Automated systems can assist in monitoring and deploying updates promptly, minimizing the window of opportunity for hackers to exploit vulnerabilities.

3. Data Encryption for Enhanced Security

Securing data at rest and in transit is paramount. Implementing encryption techniques ensures that even if unauthorized access occurs, the intercepted data remains indecipherable. This is particularly critical for sensitive information, such as personal and financial data, which, if compromised, can lead to severe consequences.

4. Network Security Measures

Protecting the network infrastructure is a cornerstone of cybersecurity. Firewalls, intrusion detection systems, and virtual private networks (VPNs) are essential components for safeguarding digital spaces. Regularly monitoring network traffic and employing advanced threat detection mechanisms contribute to the proactive identification of potential security threats.

5. Employee Training and Awareness

Human error is a significant contributor to cybersecurity breaches. Comprehensive training programs that educate employees on security best practices, the importance of strong passwords, and the dangers of phishing attacks are vital. An informed and vigilant workforce acts as an additional layer of defense against hacking attempts.

Conclusion

Securing digital spaces against hacking requires a multifaceted approach that combines technological measures with user education and awareness. Identifying and reporting cyber threats promptly, implementing robust cybersecurity best practices, and fostering a culture of vigilance are essential elements in the ongoing battle against cybercrime. As technology continues to evolve, so do the tactics employed by hackers, making it imperative for individuals and organizations to stay proactive in their efforts to protect digital assets. By collectively embracing a security-first mindset, we can create a safer and more resilient digital landscape for the future.

Introduction

In an era dominated by digital interactions and the widespread use of social media, safeguarding personal information has become a paramount concern. The rise of online threats, particularly in the form of blackmail, underscores the need for individuals to be vigilant about their privacy. This article aims to explore the various aspects of protecting personal information, from legal recourse against online threats to implementing robust privacy settings and online safety practices.

Legal Recourse Against Online Threats

In the face of online threats and blackmail attempts, understanding the legal avenues available is crucial. Blackmail is a criminal offense in many jurisdictions, and victims can pursue legal action against perpetrators. However, the effectiveness of legal recourse often depends on the nature of the threat and the jurisdiction in question.

1. Defining Blackmail

Blackmail typically involves the coercion of individuals through the threat of revealing embarrassing, disgraceful, or damaging information. Legal definitions vary, but generally, it is considered a criminal act that can lead to severe penalties for the perpetrator.

2. Reporting Incidents

Victims of blackmail should promptly report the incident to law enforcement authorities. Timely reporting enhances the chances of identifying and apprehending the perpetrator. It is crucial to provide authorities with as much information as possible, including details about the threat, the individual making it, and any evidence available.

3. Working with Law Enforcement

Collaborating with law enforcement agencies is vital for a successful resolution. Investigators may be able to trace the origin of the threat, gather evidence, and build a case against the perpetrator. Cooperation and transparency on the part of the victim can significantly aid law enforcement efforts.

4. Legal Protections

Some jurisdictions offer specific legal protections for victims of online harassment and blackmail. Understanding these protections and seeking legal advice can empower individuals to navigate the legal landscape more effectively.

Privacy Settings and Online Safety

Preventing blackmail and protecting personal information also involve proactive steps to enhance online safety. Individuals must be cognizant of the digital footprint they leave behind and take measures to safeguard their privacy.

1. Social Media Privacy Settings

One of the primary sources of personal information for potential blackmailers is social media. Adjusting privacy settings on platforms like Facebook, Twitter, and Instagram can restrict the visibility of personal details to a select audience. Users should regularly review and update these settings to align with their comfort levels.

2. Limiting Personal Information Sharing

Exercise caution when sharing personal information online. Avoid disclosing sensitive details such as home addresses, phone numbers, or financial information on public forums. Cybercriminals often exploit such information for malicious purposes.

3. Two-Factor Authentication (2FA)

Implementing two-factor authentication adds an extra layer of security to online accounts. Even if a malicious actor gains access to login credentials, 2FA requires an additional verification step, making it significantly more challenging for unauthorized individuals to compromise accounts.

4. Regularly Monitoring Online Presence

Routinely monitoring online presence can help identify any suspicious activity promptly. Regularly reviewing social media accounts, online profiles, and conducting internet searches for personal information can be part of an effective strategy to guard against potential threats.

Conclusion

In a world where personal information is increasingly vulnerable to exploitation, individuals must take proactive steps to protect themselves from blackmail and other online threats. Legal recourse, including reporting incidents and working with law enforcement, can serve as a powerful deterrent to potential perpetrators. Additionally, implementing robust privacy settings and adhering to online safety best practices can significantly reduce the risk of falling victim to blackmail.

As technology continues to evolve, so too do the methods employed by those seeking to exploit personal information for nefarious purposes. Staying informed about emerging threats and continuously adapting security measures is crucial in the ongoing effort to safeguard personal privacy. By understanding the legal landscape, utilizing privacy settings effectively, and adopting a vigilant approach to online safety, individuals can fortify their defenses against the ever-present threat of blackmail in the digital age.

In the journey through the diverse landscapes of crime and safety explored in this comprehensive guide, we have delved into the intricacies of personal security, community well-being, and the protection of our digital lives. Each chapter has been a stepping stone, unveiling strategies and practices to fortify ourselves against the various threats that loom in our modern world. As we draw the final curtain on this exploration, it is fitting to reflect on the overarching themes and principles that can collectively empower a safer future for us all.

Recap of Key Strategies and Practices for Safeguarding Against Crime

The foundation of a safer future rests upon the implementation of key strategies and practices outlined in the preceding chapters. Assault prevention, robbery deterrence, and kidnapping preparedness constitute the bedrock of personal safety. From recognizing and navigating aggressive behavior on the road to avoiding public intoxication and its consequences, the spectrum of threats is wide, and our response must be comprehensive.

The emphasis on responsible drinking, fraud awareness, identity theft protection, and safeguarding personal property underscores the importance of awareness and vigilance. Homicide risk reduction and combatting drug trafficking remind us that personal security extends beyond individual safety, intertwining with the welfare of our communities.

Encouraging Community Involvement and Awareness

A safer future is a collective endeavor, and community involvement is paramount. As we have seen in chapters addressing workplace safety, maintaining public order, and personal safety for children and teens, the strength of our communities lies in the commitment of each member to the well-being of the whole. Initiatives promoting responsible behavior, recognizing and reporting suspicious activity, and fostering a culture of safety contribute to a resilient and secure social fabric.

Through open communication, neighborhood watch programs, and educational campaigns, communities can actively participate in creating an environment where crime finds fewer opportunities to thrive. By understanding the unique challenges faced by different demographics, we can tailor our efforts to address the specific needs of our diverse society.

Inspiring a Culture of Responsibility and Safety

Creating a safer future requires a cultural shift towards responsibility and safety. Responsible drinking is not just an individual choice but a societal norm. Similarly, protecting personal information and securing digital spaces is a shared responsibility that demands a collective commitment to cybersecurity.

Inspiring this cultural transformation involves dismantling stereotypes, challenging harmful behaviors, and fostering empathy. It requires education that extends beyond the individual, reaching into homes, schools, and workplaces. By cultivating a culture that values safety, we empower individuals to make informed choices and contribute to the well-being of the entire community.

Conclusion: A Call to Action

The journey through the various dimensions of crime and safety has been both enlightening and challenging. The diverse chapters of this book have underscored the need for a holistic approach to personal security, community well-being, and digital protection. As we stand at the threshold of a safer future, it is imperative that we heed the call to action embedded in the collective knowledge we have gathered.

The conclusion of this guide is not the end but a beginning - a call to action for individuals, communities, and societies at large. It is a call to be vigilant, to be proactive, and to be responsible stewards of our safety and the safety of those around us. By embracing the strategies and practices outlined in this book, we can collectively build a future where crime is thwarted, and safety is a shared reality.

As we navigate the complexities of our modern world, let us remember that the power to create a safer future resides within each one of us. It is a power born of knowledge, fortified by awareness, and fueled by a commitment to the well-being of ourselves and our communities. In this collective endeavor, we find the promise of a future where safety is not just a goal but a lived experience - a future that we can build together, one step at a time.

"Safeguarding Against Crime in Everyday Life" is a comprehensive guide that equips readers with essential knowledge and practical strategies to enhance personal safety and security. The book explores the multifaceted landscape of crime, providing insights into its definition and societal impact. Organized into twenty insightful chapters, the book delves into various aspects of crime prevention, from assault and robbery to identity theft and digital security.

Readers will learn to recognize and avoid potentially dangerous situations, acquire self-defense techniques, and adopt safe practices for handling valuables. The book also covers topics such as road rage management, responsible drinking, fraud awareness, and community initiatives for violence prevention. With a focus on empowering individuals, the concluding chapter emphasizes the importance of community involvement and awareness, inspiring a culture of responsibility and safety for a more secure future. Whether in public spaces, online, or at home, this book provides a holistic approach to safeguarding against crime in our daily lives.

ABOUT THE AUTHOR

Mr. C. P. Kumar is a retired Scientist 'G' from National Institute of Hydrology, Roorkee, Uttarakhand, India. He is also a Reiki Healer and Chakra Balancing practitioner (with pendulum dowsing) and offers Emotional Freedom Technique (EFT) to help individuals with emotional issues. Mr. Kumar has authored many books on technical, spiritual, and social topics.

For further details, you may visit his webpage
https://www.angelfire.com/nh/cpkumar/virgo.html